Contents

Acknowledgements v

1 Introduction 1

2 Context 3
Social model of disability 3
Disability discrimination legislation 3
Reasonable adjustments 5

3 Hearing impairments and aids to hearing 6
Hearing impairment 6
Aids to hearing 8
Aids to hearing in the classroom 8

4 Communication modes 10
Spoken English 11
Sign languages 11
British Sign Language (BSL) 11
Signed English (SE) 14
Sign Supported English (SSE) 14
Lip reading 14
Cued Speech 15
Total Communication 15
Text-based communication 15
Improving the learning environment 18
Data projector 19
Interactive whiteboards, interactive whiteboard emulators
and wireless technologies 20
Adapting existing technology 20
Health and safety in the teaching and learning environment 21
Learning preferences 22
Pace 25

5 Preparing accessible teaching materials 27

Structuring learning 29

Writing style 30

Readability 31

  Chunking text 36

  Font 36

  Upper or lower case letters 37

Using digital images 37

  Digital still cameras 38

  Photo Story 3 for Windows 38

  PowerPoint storyboards 39

  Big Book Maker 40

  Clicker 5 40

  Digital video 41

  Webcams 42

  Video conferencing 43

  Digital microscopes 44

  Scanning images and objects 45

  Finding images on the web 45

  Linking to websites 45

  Flash 46

  Buying images 46

Symbols 48

Mind mapping/concept mapping 49

Using the Internet 50

Creating interactive materials 50

  Interactive whiteboard software 50

  'Hot Potatoes' 51

  Electronic voting systems 52

  'ClozePro' by Crick Software 53

  The Microsoft Office Suite 53

Supporting the deaf writer 53

  Penfriend XP 54

  WordBar 54

Learning platforms 54

References and further reading 56

Glossary 57

Acknowledgements

Many thanks to the following organisations:

> Walsall Adult Education Service for permission to use a screenshot of their Learning Platform website.
> Widgit Software for the Writing with Symbols 2000 website screenshot; Writing with Symbols 2000 and Widgit Rebus symbols ©Widgit Software Tel: 01223 425558 Web: http://www.widgit.com/.
> Wolverhampton University for their permission to include screenshots of their Artsigns website, http://www.artsigns.ac.uk/.
> Half-Baked Software for their kind permission to use a screenshot of the Hot Potatoes website.
> CHANGE for permission to use a selection symbols from their Change Picture Bank; information on http://www.changepeople.co.uk .
> Microsoft product screen shots reprinted with permission from Microsoft Corporation.
> Action on Deafness (Leicester)
> The Royal National Institute for the Deaf

Photo: Sue Parkins, NIACE

The term 'deaf' will be used throughout this publication to refer to a person with any degree of deafness.

1

Introduction

Around nine million people in the UK are known to have a hearing loss of some kind. The true number is likely to be even higher, as many of us are reluctant to seek help for hearing difficulties and indeed may not even be aware that our hearing has deteriorated.

Hearing loss can be experienced by anyone. If we have not been born deaf we may lose hearing as a result of an illness such as meningitis or rubella; through a simple medical condition such as an ear infection; gradually acquire hearing difficulties as we get older; or suddenly as the result of an accident.

The age at which a person loses hearing and the degree of hearing loss are two of the factors which influence literacy levels and impact upon language development, access to education and information, motivation, feelings of self worth and social and emotional well being.

> Ninety-five per cent of profoundly deaf school-leavers only reach a reading-age of nine. This functional illiteracy means that even the nuances of stories from basic tabloid newspapers are beyond the reach of many deaf adults.
> Dr Abram Stern, Institute of Psychiatry, King's College London, in Literacy Today:
> **http://www.literacytrust.org.uk/pubs/stern.htm**

However, someone who loses their hearing in later life may have a high literacy level but still experience the same feelings of isolation and frustration as a result of feeling excluded. Communication challenges may leave the deaf person feeling unable to participate in group activities or in some cases, communicate effectively on a 1:1 basis. This can be true of those with even a fairly mild hearing loss as, once they have lost the thread of a conversation, they can become confused. The pace of the hearing world is frequently inappropriate for those who require time to assimilate information and may need

1

frequent repetition and clarification. Misunderstandings are commonplace and teachers must find ways of checking a deaf person's learning if they are to take remedial action

Education has historically failed many deaf learners, but today's climate, in terms of enlightened attitudes, legislation and enabling technologies, makes for much more accessible learning. Yesterday's school 'failures' may be today's successful adult learners and there will be many who will benefit enormously from lifelong learning. This book will look at the ways in which technology can be used to support teaching and learning for deaf people, enabling them to access the skills and knowledge they need as teachers, learners and workers, and also help to ensure that participation is enjoyable and enriching.

This e-guideline will put the use of technology into context by exploring what hearing loss or impairment means, its implications in terms of teaching and learning and the impact of the Disability Discrimination Act. It will focus on dismantling barriers to learning by looking at the ways in which technology can support communication and interpretation, the learning environment, and access to teaching and learning materials. Examples will indicate how technology can be put into useful practice.

Both teachers and learners with hearing impairments have informed the content of this publication by sharing their knowledge and experience. We intend this book to be useful to you if you are a learner, a teacher, other education staff member or someone interested in using technology in the learning environment.

Photo: Sue Parkins, NIACE

2

Context

Social model of disability

It is important to avoid a 'medical model' approach to disability; that is focusing on the impairment as the cause of any challenges that deaf people are experiencing. Rather, we shall take a 'social model' approach, recognising that barriers experienced by people with disabilities, including barriers to accessing services, are erected by society itself. Barriers may include physical obstacles, lack of knowledge and skills, attitudes of others, and employment opportunities for disabled people. So, for example, in the past the physical environment of education provision has not been constructed to take account of the access requirements of people with sensory or physical impairments. Further, the training of teachers rarely included instruction on how to teach in inclusive ways by, for example, making learning materials and delivery accessible to deaf learners. Finally, only recently with the introduction of the Disability Discrimination Act and Disability Equality Duty have learning providers had to consider seriously how they make provision accessible to both staff and learners.

Disability discrimination legislation

The Disability Discrimination Act (DDA) was passed in 1995, followed by the DDA part 4 (Special Educational Needs and Disability Act – 'SENDA 2001') and later the DDA (2005) that brought in the Disability Equality Duty.

The DDA made it unlawful to discriminate against a person on the basis of their disability. The DDA part 4 legislation brought in specific duties for education providers.

The legislation is anticipatory, which means that organisations should anticipate the likely requirements of any disabled learners as well as respond to individual requirements as they arise.

It would be naïve to think that a learning provider has no deaf or hard-of-hearing learners, staff or visitors. It is, therefore, incumbent on providers to consider, with disabled people, how they will make their services accessible and inclusive. Preparations should include ensuring that staff members are trained and knowledgeable about how to include and involve people with disabilities in all the services they provide.

Most importantly, it should never be assumed that people who have hearing impairments have the same needs or that one piece of equipment or the recruitment of signers will break down all the teaching and learning barriers they could experience. Deaf learners will need to be treated as individuals with individual requirements and it is essential that every deaf learner is encouraged to discuss specific needs throughout a course.

Important anticipatory actions checklist

> Have all staff members had disability and deaf awareness training?
> Are staff members aware of the range of technological and human support they could offer to deaf people?
> Are staff members aware of the range of individual hearing aids that a learner may be using?
> Do front-line staff know what to do if a deaf learner contacts them?
> Are there always staff members on duty who know how to operate a text phone?
> Do you know where to contact trained communication support workers or sign language interpreters?
> Do rooms have loop systems installed? If not, do you have a portable loop available?
> Do all staff know how to facilitate good communication practices?

Reasonable adjustments

The Disability Discrimination Act also requires education providers to make reasonable adjustments to ensure that disabled learners can access provision. It is not possible to list reasonable adjustments per se; a reasonable adjustment is what enables an individual to be fully involved in an appropriate learning activity. It is highly likely that each individual will require different things. One learner with a hearing impairment may require a Communication Support Worker, another, subtitles to all DVD material used; someone else may need key words and phrases explained.

Making reasonable adjustments – Supporting deaf teachers resource

All staff members have anxieties and questions that need clarifying when they start a new job or begin working in a different site. Action Deafness has prepared a Tutor Support Pack, aimed at deaf BSL tutors. This guides the tutor through the sort of things they need to know and general questions they might want to ask, such as access to buildings, communicating with line managers, matters of health and safety, preparing to teach adults, course and teaching planning, progress and achievement and Inspection. The pack includes an easy-to-understand written document, a BSL DVD, and a resource CD ROM with templates for tutor use.

3

Hearing impairments and aids to hearing

Hearing impairment

Definitions of deafness

The following definitions are taken from the Royal National Institute for the Deaf (RNID) website

> **Deaf people**
> We use the term deaf people in a general way when we are talking about people with all degrees of deafness. Used with a capital D it often denotes a profoundly deaf person who may have British Sign Language as their first or preferred language.

> **Hard of hearing people**
> We use the term hard of hearing to describe people with a mild to severe hearing loss. We quite often use it to describe people who have lost their hearing gradually. Many people in this category may use or gain some benefit from hearing aids.

> **Deafened people**
> People who were born hearing and became severely or profoundly deaf after learning to speak are often described as deafened. This can happen suddenly or gradually.

> **Deafblind people**
> Many deafblind people have some hearing and vision. Others will be totally deaf and totally blind. There are about 23,000 deafblind people in the UK.

> **The deaf community**
> Many deaf people whose first or preferred language is British Sign Language (BSL) consider themselves part of the deaf community. They may describe themselves as Deaf with a capital D to emphasise their deaf identity.

http://www.rnid.org.uk

Levels of deafness

Defined according to the quietest sound you can hear, measured in decibels.

> **Mild deafness**
>
> If you have mild deafness it can cause some difficulty following speech, mainly in noisy situations. The quietest sounds you can hear are 25 to 39 decibels.

> **Moderate deafness**
>
> People with moderate deafness may have difficulty following speech without a hearing aid, and find the quietest sounds they can hear are 40 to 69 decibels.

> **Severe deafness**
>
> People with severe deafness rely a lot on lipreading, even with a hearing aid, as the quietest sounds they can hear are 70 to 94 decibels. BSL may be their first or preferred language.

> **Profound deafness**
>
> The quietest sounds that profoundly deaf people can hear average 95 decibels or more. BSL may be their first or preferred language but some prefer to lipread.

http://www.rnid.org.uk

When this chapter examines the terminology used to describe hearing loss, it is not intending to oppose the social model of disability but rather to increase understanding and dismantle the blocks and barriers to successful teaching and learning.

Hearing impairments can be usefully diagnosed and described medically. Trained audiologists will be able to measure the extent of an individual's hearing impairment and diagnosis can help lead to an assessment of how any residual hearing can be usefully augmented or improved by specialised technologies.

Whilst these terms help us to understand the different hearing impairment conditions, *they should not be used to label individuals*. Nor should it be assumed that all hearing-impaired learners require the same learning opportunities or specialist provision. Individual learners need to be assessed in order to assert the nature of their needs and what teaching materials/strategies are appropriate. As with all teaching and learning activity, there needs to be a shared understanding of what is possible and what can be delivered with the right adjustments in place.

> ## Consider
> How can you identify the impact that the teaching and learning environment might have on people who have hearing impairments?

Aids to hearing

Technology can augment the hearing of many deaf individuals. Sound amplification devices such as hearing aids are becoming more and more sophisticated and there is also a steady rise in the number of cochlear implants. These aids do not cure deafness but they can make some sounds louder. In many circumstances this may be advantageous, but a learner may have legitimate concerns when using a hearing aid within a learning environment. Ambient noise can cause problems as it is amplified alongside the noises that the learner wants to hear. Noisy technology can be an annoyance, as can chairs scraping on an uncarpeted floor. It is important that teachers do not assume that a hearing aid diminishes the challenges faced by a deaf learner and that the individual learner is consulted in a sensitive way about what they can hear and general communication issues.

Aids to hearing in the classroom

Soundfield systems utilise a microphone and speakers to amplify the voice. The wearing of radio aids, together with the use of a soundfield system, can significantly improve the learners experience and help minimise the impact of background noises.

Hearing loop systems are helpful to those individuals who use a hearing aid or a loop listening aid switched to the T setting. The loop picks up and transmits sounds to hearing aids. Different loop systems meet a range of requirements from small classrooms, where a portable system may be most appropriate, to much larger venues, where static systems should be installed. Be aware that electrical equipment may interfere with the quality of sound transmitted.

Infrared systems require learners to wear an appropriate infrared receiver. There are two types: one to suit the needs of the person with sufficient residual hearing and no aids, and one for the hearing aid wearer. There are also static and portable systems to suit the organisation's needs. Infrared is less prone to interference, providing the equipment is well cared for.

Personal listening devices can enhance sounds to neckloops, headphones including earbuds or transmit them to hearing aids. These are generally small, portable devices that can be used in a variety of settings, for example to listen to conversations in a car or restaurant, to listen to a lecture or to hear general conversations more clearly. Various microphone devices can be placed near to the source of sound that the individual wants to focus on – this might be another person, the radio, or the television.

A radio microphone system requires the learner to access the voice of the speaker via a hearing aid or cochlear implant. The speaker wears a clip-on microphone that transmits the sound to the receiver. The microphone will need to be passed on to other speakers if the learner is to pick up other voices. The advantages are that background noise interference is reduced; the disadvantage is that the receiver only picks up the sounds of the person wearing the microphone.

A conversor radio microphone system may be more appropriate for some learners. It makes use of a hand-held microphone and a neckloop receiver. This is suitable for learners who do not wear hearing aids.

Generally, these listening devices can be used by people who have a severe hearing loss or use a hearing aid with a T switch, but not for those with profound hearing loss (see 'levels of deafness' on page 7).

4
Communication modes

The communication approaches used by deaf individuals depend on a number of factors.

Age of hearing loss: Individuals who are born deaf or who become deaf in infancy, before they acquired spoken language skills, are referred to as pre-lingually deaf. People who have acquired a hearing impairment due to age, an injury, an infection, or a degenerating condition may retain their speech but need to learn other ways of receiving communication.

Exposure to communication systems: Opportunities to develop signed, spoken, or written language depend very much on individual circumstances. Family influences will inevitably have impacted upon the adult learner's communication, as will school experiences. Educational philosophies vary in their acceptance of British Sign Language as a teaching tool, with some schools and local authorities promoting mainly lip reading and English-based communication approaches. The quality of an adult's past language experience, whether signed or spoken, will affect their communication with hearing and deaf people.

Professional support: The knowledge and skills of health, social care, and other professional staff to signpost young people and adults to opportunities to learn communication methods will have impacted upon communication skills.

The individual: Individuals will react differently to their hearing loss and will develop coping strategies. Adults, in particular, are often reluctant to acknowledge and seek help for any difficulties with hearing. Coping strategies may vary from seeking help, to withdrawal from social situations that could expose their difficulties.

Other people: Deaf people may have to adapt their communication to respond to the attitudes and reactions of others to their hearing impairment. Their social environment and exposure to deaf and hearing people will have impacted upon confidence and competence.

Spoken English

There will be many deaf learners who have good, clear speech and others whose speech is more difficult to follow or who choose not to use their voice. There will be those who are reluctant to use their voice in unfamiliar environments or in front of strangers but may be happy in familiar or one-to-one situations.

Sign languages

These are forms of communication that generally rely on physical hand gestures, including finger-spelling. According to the Ethnologue report (http://www.ethnologue.com) there are 121 deaf sign languages used worldwide.

British Sign Language (BSL)

BSL is used not only within the UK but is also taught as an additional language for deaf children in some European countries. There is no universal sign language and even countries sharing a common spoken language, for example in English-speaking America and Britain, will have developed their own sign language. American and British Sign Language (ASL and BSL) are therefore distinct languages.

Signed language does not have the same grammatical structure as spoken languages. BSL is not a literal translation of each spoken or written word, but a language in its own right, with its own visual grammar, syntax, and vocabulary, and is now recognised as a modern language alongside spoken languages such as French, Spanish, and Japanese.

People who use BSL as their first or preferred language may experience difficulties with the literal interpretation of spoken or written words that are ambiguous or have double meanings. For example a phrase such as 'learning journey' in educational terms means the types of learning experiences, courses and qualifications a learner has undertaken to get to the point they are at now. It could also mean the bus or walk to the college or learning centre. English is full of words that have more than one meaning and can lead to confusion and misunderstandings. The common use of non-literal English can be confusing for deaf learners who may need a literal translation. For example, idioms such as 'go the extra mile' or 'flogging a dead horse' may be unfamiliar expressions that leave a learner bewildered.

New words, especially in the rapidly advancing world of technology often require new signs and interpretations. Some terms like CD and DVD are generally finger-spelt, others are designated a sign. Some new signs develop locally in response to an immediate need to use the word. These signs, which may be different in other areas of the country or with different groups of people, are known as dialects, much like the different regional dialects in spoken English. It is therefore possible that a learner may not always use the same signs as those presented to him/her and may need further explanation to enable clear understanding.

Signing on DVDs, videos, signed interpretation on national television and inclusive educational practices have all helped to standardise signs and overcome issues surrounding sign dialect. In some cases specific DVDs or CD-ROMS have or are being prepared to help deaf learners access curriculum areas. For example the RNID with the HBOS Foundation are producing a Financial Literacy pack and a dictionary of financial terms in BSL. (**http://www.rnid.org.uk**).

The University of Wolverhampton has developed its own online glossaries for several of its science and engineering courses. These sites list keywords, terms and phrases that are used or useful within the specified curriculum areas. These words are then defined in written English and a video clip of a BSL interpreter signing the word is shown.

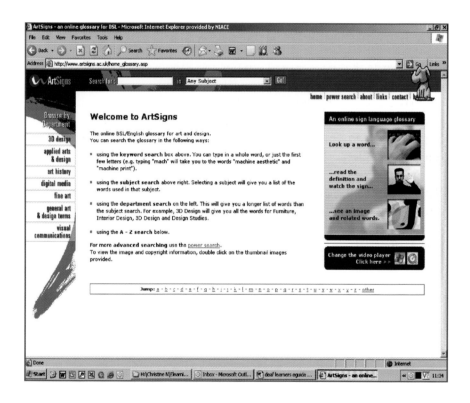

Online glossaries

http://www.artsigns.ac.uk
http://www.sciencesigns.ac.uk
http://www.engineeringsigns.ac.uk

Signed English (SE)

SE is a communication method that follows the grammar and syntax of English. It takes signs from BSL, finger-spelling, and generated signs in order to provide signing to support each English word as it is spoken. It deals with specific aspects of English, such as plurals and auxiliary verbs that are not in the visual spatial language. A plural in BSL would be clarified by a repetition of a sign, so 'trees' would be a repetition of the sign for 'tree'; in SE a plural may be a sign followed by a finger-spelt 's'. SE is often used by teachers to develop English-language skills.

Sign Supported English (SSE)

This is based on spoken English with the use of BSL signs to aid communication. Unlike SE, this form of communication does not try to closely follow each English word but offers support for the most significant words. Learners will use more English than BSL or vice versa depending upon their linguistic abilities.

Lip reading

Some deaf people are excellent lip readers given the right circumstances, but it is not a reliable form of communication and can lead to misunderstanding and failure to access important information. Lip reading competence is linked to understanding of English and to the way in which the speaker enunciates words. Even a clear speaker will not be able to distinguish between words that have the same lip pattern, like *big* and *pig*. It is also very demanding of the deaf person's concentration and therefore very tiring. Within a learning environment it can be especially difficult as people move and may not be facing the learner at crucial times.

Cued speech

Cued speech is used as a way to clarify lip patterns. A hand shape and position near the mouth is used to differentiate sounds. This may be used by specially trained communicators.

Total Communication

It is important to recognise that adults may use a combination of the most appropriate and useful communication methods to understand and be understood. This is referred to as 'Total Communication'. The languages and methods used might include British Sign Language (BSL), Signed English (SE), gesture, visual cues, spoken English, written English, and the preferred language of family members if this is not English.

Using Total Communication

Poole Adult and Community Learning actively use Total Communication. Tutors across all curriculum areas are encouraged to undertake training and use total communication to support their teaching. Total Communication is the using of any means of communication, including voice, sign language, finger-spelling, lipreading, amplification, writing, gesture and visual imagery. It is used in response to the individual's needs.

Text-based communication

There will be learners who like to use pen and paper to communicate, and this can be very useful. Deaf learners may be very familiar with text phones, having used them before the mobile phone became widely available. They may be using text phones on a land line at home and have their own shorthand. Online chat does not require listening skills and is an inclusive activity for many deaf learners.

Digital messaging has revolutionised communication, from pagers, text, and mobile phones to email and instant messaging applications. All can be used to support the teaching and learning experiences of hearing impaired people.

Messaging can be used for one-off communications via pagers or mobile phones to:

> remind learners about a change in timetable or venue;

> inform them about homework or assignment titles;

> let them know that someone wants their attention – this is particularly useful when learners are either working in noisy environments or outside working in land-based areas.

Digital messaging can particularly support hearing-impaired learners, by equalising the communication medium, with other non-hearing-impaired learners. If, for example, the teacher tells the learners that the next tutorial will be conducted by email or instant messaging, the barriers to participation change: from auditory barriers to literacy, ICT and Internet access barriers.

Case Study: Using online chat in a food hygiene course

The tutor wanted a discussion session that would be more inclusive for the deaf learner in the group, who had hitherto found it very difficult to engage in such activity. The strain of keeping up at such times put her under a lot of stress and she told the tutor that she stopped trying.

The tutor gave out an agenda a week ahead of the planned online chat that outlined specific things to be discussed during the session and asked for a chat area on the college Moodle.

The session worked well and the learner was able to follow the discussion and make valuable contributions that reflected her understanding. The technology meant that her hearing loss was no barrier to the discussion.

E-mail also empowers deaf learners. It is quick, allows for easy editing for learners who find writing a challenge, and can incorporate images and other explanatory attachments. It can also be a useful tool to develop literacy skills. E-mails have the advantage of giving participants the opportunity to think about what they want to say, compose it and reply once they have reflected on messages sent to them. By contrast instant messaging such as MSN has the advantage of operating immediately like a conversation: two or more participants can be live and online, communicating in real time. Online messaging has been used to conduct research questioning with people with disabilities (Anderberg and Jonsson, 2005). Using this approach avoids the pitfalls of stand-alone questionnaires and gains some of the flexibility afforded by more open interview schedules where misunderstandings and lack of clarity can be addressed immediately. The disadvantages are that learners who need time to type or think about their responses may get left behind in a conversation that has moved on.

Case Study: E-mail buddies

A basic skills tutor worked with several deaf learners whose first language was BSL and who were developing their written English skills. He wanted to establish some real-world communication that would have a life of its own, not simply rely on session time and restrict what could be done there. So, he set up each deaf learner with a hearing learner they had never met but who had good English skills and could communicate effectively with the deaf learners. The aim was to find out about each other, to ask and respond to questions.

This proved highly motivational and did indeed develop reading and writing skills, including the organisation of text and understanding of the conventions used. As planned, the communication eventually moved outside the session time, becoming more of a social activity, but with clear educational benefits as there was a real incentive to read and write English.

Improving the learning environment

Barriers to learning are created by practitioners who are unaware of practices and environmental factors that exclude deaf people. Tutors need to be aware, for example, that their clothing, jewellery or untrimmed facial hair can interfere with communication, as can standing or sitting with the light source behind a speaker, or speakers holding papers near to their faces.

Deaf awareness training is a pre-requisite to getting it right, and the technology then provides many of the tools that lead from awareness to more fully inclusive practice.

Poor acoustics and lighting, and unsuitable seating layouts, can create huge barriers for deaf learners. People who have mild hearing loss and those who enhance their hearing with hearing aids can experience difficulties if there are other external noises. Loud chatter in the corridor, mowing machines or heavy vehicles manoeuvring outside, other learners conversing in class or chairs scraping across the floor, can prevent people who are deaf from hearing the sound they are trying to focus on. Unfortunately, hearing aids do not just promote the sound the user wants to hear, but amplify a range of sounds, including unwanted background noises. As a result, users have been known to switch off their aids.

Communication can be impeded by:

> **Poor or low lighting levels**: faces or objects cannot be seen clearly;

> **Bright light**, including sunlight, shining behind the head of the speaker: this throws the face into deep shadow.
Bright light will also affect the clarity of images displayed by data projectors. It is important, therefore, to ensure that hearing-impaired learners are not placed in the difficult situation of reading projected images with dimmed lights and trying to watch a speaker at the same time.

> **Room layouts**, where deaf people cannot see the faces of others in the room, for example where learners are sitting in rows or grouped around tables (cabaret style). Deaf people who use sign language interpreters may have issues locating the speaker and the interpreter. Seating arranged in horseshoe shapes tends to work well.

> **Failing to ensure that individual learners are catered for** in terms of any personal aids that are being used.

Data projector

Teachers use data projectors to project computer -based information on to a screen, wall or interactive whiteboard. The advantages for deaf learners are:

> A range of multi-media resources can be prepared and made clearly visible to the whole group, and audible to some deaf learners;

> The tutor can navigate between resources on a mouse click, including notes made and saved during previous sessions.

> More inclusive practice: the tutor can stand/sit next to the projected information enabling the learner to see the tutor's face and so know when s/he is talking, see expressions and lip read.

If learners are seated in a horseshoe around the screen/board they can see the tutor, the information and other members of the group. This is a less stressful situation.

Beware of noisy technologies such as older data projectors and air conditioning systems and make sure that any aural information is transmitted through good-quality speakers.

Interactive whiteboards, interactive whiteboard emulators and wireless technologies

Some hardware offers opportunities for interactivity in a whole-class/group situation. Interactive whiteboards and whiteboard emulators are excellent, but there are some disadvantages for the deaf learner. A tutor or learner may be talking whilst working at the board, back towards the group, and this can cause the deaf member to miss out on significant information. It may be better to opt for wireless technologies that enable tutors and learners to interact without moving from their seats. A wireless mouse, keyboard, graphics tablet or more sophisticated tablets such as the Interwrite or the Smart Airliner, are all significant aids to ensuring the inclusion of deaf learners. These can be passed around a group for them to interact with projected information and, a horseshoe seating arrangement means that they can track users more easily.

Adapting existing technology

Many learning providers use digital technologies originally designed for specialised professional or general public markets, for example, vibrating pagers to send alerts or messages to deaf learners. Clocks or timers that flash or light up can be successfully used by learners needing to time specific activities such as a scientific experiment or their cooking. Flashing lights can also be used to get the attention of deaf learners engrossed in an activity. The Accessibility options on personal computers allow the user to choose more appropriate text or visual alternatives to system sounds, such as flashing the caption bar, or active screen or desktop.

Case study – Taking blood pressure measurements

Until recently all blood pressure measurements were taken manually, by listening through a stethoscope, reading a silver mercury measure and manipulating the air valve on an inflatable cuff. Electronic devices, sometimes called 'Wellness kits' can now measure these with great accuracy and provide a digital reading. This equipment has been successfully used by deaf learners at Stubbing Court, an equine work-based learning provider, in Chesterfield. Here they have adapted existing technology, a type of wellness kit, to measure the pulse and blood pressure of horses. By attaching a large strap to the equipment they can secure the monitor onto the horse's chest and obtain the readings they need to complete the horse's health assessment.

Consider:

> How can you ensure that the rooms you work or learn in are free from extraneous and distracting noises?

> How do you monitor other environmental conditions such as lighting and seating arrangements?

> Are staff members aware of factors impeding communication for deaf learners?

> What facilities and enabling technologies do you have for deaf learners?

Health and safety in the teaching and learning environment

Learners who are deaf or hearing impaired may not be able to access or understand the same auditory cues as other learners. It is crucial to deal with this to maintain a safe environment in which to learn. Obvious hazards are warning alarms, such as those sounded for: fire bells, reversing vehicles, moving machinery and lowered shutters. Others may include verbal, urgent instructions or warnings given by teachers or learners for example, warning that someone is carrying boiling water or sharp knives across a busy training kitchen.

Fire alarms

Birmingham Rathbone run busy E2E training programmes for learners with learning difficulties. Some of the learners have hearing impairments. Until recently the fire alarm was auditory only. During the regular tests and drills the learners who had partial hearing responded, partly because the bell was so loud that they could hear it, and partly because it created a vibration in the air powerful enough to shake one of the partition walls. Birmingham Rathbone has reviewed the alarm system and will be changing to one that is both auditory and visual, that is, having clear flashing/strobe lights.

Consider:

> What do you have in your learning environment that sends out auditory warning noises?

> How would a learner with hearing impairments be warned?

> What adjustments can you put in place to ensure that deaf or partially hearing learners are not put at risk or disadvantaged by auditory warnings?

Learning preferences

Each learner will have some preferences about how they learn. It may be a preference for formal or informal styles, for learning alone or with others. Preferences are, of course, changeable and often dependent on the subject or context of the learning.Four main, though not exclusive modes are: visual, auditory, reading/writing and kinaesthetic.

Four ways of learning

Visual

Learners who have visual learning preferences may prefer to pay close attention to the body language and movements of teachers/practitioners and other learners. Visual learners may think in pictures. They prefer supporting material to be illustrated, contain graphs and diagrams.

Auditory

Learners with auditory learning preferences, learn well through listening. They like to have instructions described to them and will often pay particular attention to the tone pitch and speed of what is said.

Kinaesthetic

Learners with kinaesthetic preferences learn through doing. They prefer action and activities. They may prefer to try things out, engage in role-play and have real objects to touch and experiment with.

Reading and writing

Learners with this preference like to look things up, refer to reference materials such as dictionaries, textbooks and the Internet. They also prefer to write things down and may take very detailed notes.

Most of us employ a mixture of these, but may have a tendency to use one or two in particular. deaf learners will have their own individual preferences.

Technology has given teachers and learners the freedom to easily use interactive and multi-media resources within and beyond the classroom. We can therefore address a range of preferred learning styles within one session and accommodate the special needs of a range of deaf learners.

Few individuals who are deaf are likely to benefit *fully* from auditory teaching approaches. However, there will be progressively more deaf people benefiting from increasingly sophisticated hearing aids and implants. Teachers can make effective use of residual hearing by creating resources encompassing superior sound clips delivered through good quality speakers or headphones.

Case study: Key word dictionaries

A deaf learner was struggling to keep pace with the new vocabulary introduced each week so the tutor made a PowerPoint presentation of key words and phrases. The words were typed in comic sans, font size 32 and longer words were also re-typed in syllables that were animated on a click to make up the whole word. With help, the learner was then able to practise articulating the words. Most words had a picture and some had a brief signed explanation (filmed with a digital still camera that has the facility to record short video clips) and some provided additional text information. The teacher added a sound file to each slide so that the learner could listen to the correct pronunciation. The learner was provided with a print and electronic copy which allowed for preparation before the class and post-class support and revision.

Deaf learners who do not use English as their first or second language are unlikely to prefer reading and writing, but the deaf learner may be aiming to develop literacy skills or needs to work with some text-based materials. Technology gives teachers the means to create electronic resources that can be adapted to make them less text-heavy and more visual.

Case study

V is a deaf Iraqi learner whose first language is Arabic. He studies on a full-time ESOL course and has studied British Sign Language (BSL) since arriving in the UK. He lip-reads a little and uses some speech. He has a communication support worker (CSW) who supports him in class and also works with him on a one-to-one basis for two hours per week. He finds it more meaningful to see information than to try and listen. Consequently, he finds it much easier to take in information if he can have handouts to read before a class. He finds it helpful when certain things are translated into Arabic (for example, grammatical explanations). He finds information on 'posters' around the room and diagrams and charts helpful. He likes to learn with his peers and participates actively in a small group in a quiet environment when others take turns to speak, so he can take in everything. He loves to use computers and surfs the Web with appropriate guidance and support.

He will spend hours working on reading comprehensions, which are based on texts found on the Web, particularly if they are about politics and the Middle East.

From the 'ESOL Access for All' guidance (DfES, 2006:12)

Pace

Keeping pace with a class of hearing people may provide a real challenge for deaf learners. It is very important that tutors keep control of the learning environment and, when presenting new information, ensure that the subject under discussion does not change without checking the deaf learner understands there has been a shift. It is a good idea to present the aims of the session electronically, indicate when things have moved on and use the technology to note any new and significant information that may arise. This can be saved for future reference, for revision and to clarify any confusion.

One of the greatest advantages of using technology with deaf learners is that it allows them more time to assimilate new information. More time and more accessible resources means, in theory, that they can prepare for a session and re-visit learning, working either independently or with support staff. Non-linear learning means that the student is not restricted to the one off classroom-based session but can access saved electronic resources. Likewise, the teacher can sensitively toggle between past and present resources within a session to ensure that the learner has not missed something vital.

Out-of-class access to resources can be supplied electronically via VLE/intranet, portable storage, email or by providing printed materials.

Consider

> How do teaching approaches take account of different learning preferences?

> How do teaching staff in your provision ensure they don't create barriers to participation for deaf learners?

Case study – using a PDA to support a deaf student mechanic

R is profoundly deaf. Although the spoken language at home is not English he uses BSL as his first language. R wanted to become a car mechanic so he enrolled on a vocational course and obtained a work placement. Whilst enjoying the practical work he struggled with the new technical language. Desperate to succeed, the only way R could cope was to ask his new colleagues to write the words down on a piece of paper that he shared each week with his tutor.

The technological answer would be to provide R with an interpretation resource as and when he needed it at his work placement. A hand-held Personal Digital Assistant (PDA) is small enough to be carried to work and could enable the learner to open prepared resources that explain technical terms using text, still and moving images, and BSL clips. The learner could also use a camera function to record images of things that required explanation and take these into college so that the resource bank could be further expanded.

5

Preparing accessible teaching materials

The reading and comprehension of texts can be significantly inhibited by a failure to address issues of content, style, vocabulary, font type, and presentation. Learners who are pre-lingually deaf are likely to have experienced severe language delay that may not have been successfully addressed. Those who lost hearing in early childhood are also likely to find their use and understanding of English is affected. It is important to remember that reading and comprehension texts must be designed to provide the appropriate learning experience in an accessible way. Deaf learners need the same information to be presented in a way that respects their needs.

Technology provides teachers with tools to create high-quality teaching materials, and the means to adapt and differentiate to facilitate inclusive practice. Teachers should be aware of accessibility issues for deaf learners, carefully vet any written information before it is given and make reasonable adjustments. These adjustments may be adding images, breaking text into manageable chunks, writing in plain English, and presenting in a deaf-friendly way.

Manuals are frequently full of technical language and dense text which is inappropriate for learners with limited literacy skills. Some 'on-screen' instructions to develop IT skills will fall into this category, and teachers should consider creating very visual resources to cater for those who need more accessible instructions.

Case study: Using the animation facility in PowerPoint to teach ICT

An ICT teacher discovered that he could create PowerPoint presentations to teach deaf learners how to use a variety of software. Screen grabs, animated arrows and simple, clear text were used to guide the learners through the steps required. Each presentation was displayed on screen via a data projector and proved much easier to see and follow than actually showing each step within the different software packages. The teacher also printed the slides to create easy to follow manuals and laminated displays.

Both on-screen presentations and the manuals were later used successfully in the teaching of hearing adults.

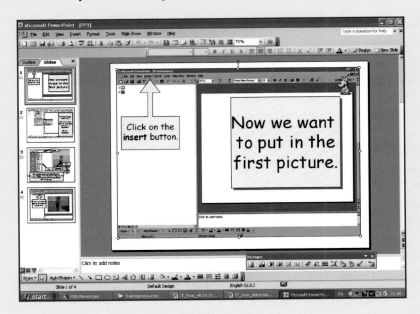

Case study: Recording a process – Smart Notebook software

Some programs, such as Smart Notebook, have the facility to record an on-screen process in any program. Typical uses for this facility might be recording how to insert an image in Microsoft Word or a mathematical process as it is written. The recorder will capture the process as it is displayed on the screen, and this can be played back as and when required. This means that the deaf learner can revisit a range of processes and the relevant vocabulary can be built up at an appropriate pace.

Be aware that this will create large (memory) files.
Smart Notebook software is freely downloadable but users have to agree to use it only with Smart Technologies products (see **http://smarttech.com/**).

If you have some other supplier's whiteboard or whiteboard emulator software check to see if it has a 'Record' option

Camtasia Studio from Tech Smith will provide quality screen recordings and the facilities to create a range of resources. Tutorials, demonstrations and presentations look professional and can incorporate high-quality sound for those deaf learners who are able to receive and benefit from aural information. View examples at: **http://www.techsmith.com**.

Structuring learning

Well planned schemes of work and session plans will show the aims and learning objectives. The content of any teaching materials should support these aims and objectives by embedding, reinforcing, illustrating or extending the key messages or learning points. Teachers must now address the issue of accessibility for a range of learners and make 'reasonable adjustments' as required by the DDA.

The content of a session will guide the use of resources and the order in which they are presented. Deaf learners need learning that is presented in a clear, logical sequence. They need to know the subject under discussion and it should be made absolutely obvious when the subject changes. All resources should be geared to introducing learning step by step, and technology offers the easiest solution. Everything needed for a session can be organised to present to the learners. Programs can be opened and minimised at the bottom of a screen or documents can be linked. Teachers can use software to display, explain concepts, model answers, make notes or annotate presentations and all of this can be saved. Once the deaf learner has understood the subject, everything is in place to facilitate independent or class based revision whereby resources can be accessed as required.

Hard copy resources can be printed in advance or, if printers are available, during the session. Many of the on-screen resources can be printed and they will therefore mirror those used in a session. Offering something that is familiar will reinforce the learning experience.

Writing style

Anything presented on screen should be clear and presented in plain English: the only exception to this would be where a piece of original text is being examined or learners are looking at the use of language. If this is the case there will need to be an accessible explanation. This explanation may be in sign, text or both and given to the whole group or an individual as appropriate.

Source texts may need to be simplified for some deaf learners or broken down and explained, and specialist vocabulary will need to be taught.

An appropriate style should be adopted: bullet points will often suffice to meet the aims and objectives. This does not mean that some learners should not be directed to extension materials that are more demanding in terms of style and readability.

Likewise with hard copy materials: adopt a style that will enable learners to access the main teaching points. This may mean differentiated worksheets or additional resources to meet particular needs. Whilst some may cope with complex sentences and a more elaborate style, others may learn better from a list of bullet points and supportive images.

Readability

As a teacher it is important to know at what level learners are reading, and to be aware of the style and complexity of texts we are presenting to them. There are a number of ways to check the 'readability' of texts. One method that can be done easily through a manual approach is the SMOG Readability Formula (see Glossary). Like most readability assessments, the SMOG index is looking for indicators of complexity, that may include sentence length and number of multi-syllable words, within a text. However the calculation is done, and SMOG is one of the easiest to do manually, the outcome is a numerical score. The score will inform you of the level of education readers would be expected to have attained to be able to read and understand the text.

SMOG readability formula

> Select a text
> Count 10 sentences.
> Count number of words that have three or more syllables.
> Multiply this by three.
> Circle the number closest to your answer:
  1 4 9 25 36 49 64 81 100 121 144 169
> Find the square root of the number you circled.
> Add 8.

This is the readability score.

Key to readability level
> 17+ unreadable
> 16 graduate level
> 13 A-level/GNVQ Advanced/NVQ 3/4
> 11 GCSE/GNVQ Intermediate/NVQ 2
> 9 Non-qualified school leaver/GNVQ Foundation/NVQ1

Online tools

There are online tools that can calculate a SMOG score:
http://linda-andrews.com/readability_tool.htm.

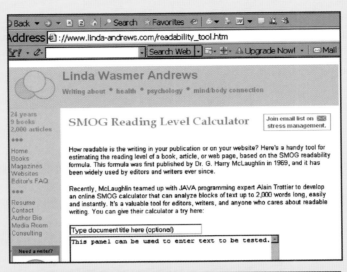

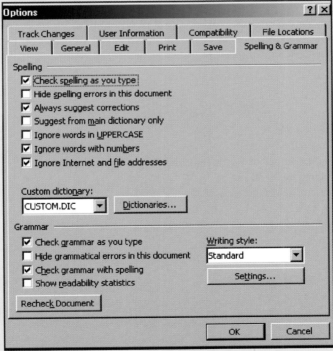

Another measure of readability is readability is the Flesch/ Flesch–Kincaid score. Microsoft Word has the facility to calculate this score.

To measure readability in Microsoft Word

First click on 'Tools' and select 'Options'. Then choose the 'Spelling and grammar' tab.

Check the boxes that say 'Check grammar with spelling' and 'Show readability statistics'. Then click OK. The next time that you do a spelling and grammar check (Go to Tools, then select 'Spelling and grammar', or press F7), a dialogue box will appear at the end of the check informing you of the Flesch Reading Ease and the Flesch–Kincaid Grade Level readability statistics for the passage checked.

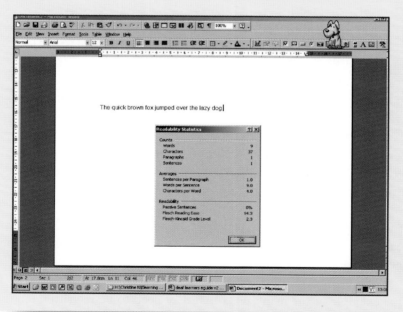

Flesch/Flesch–Kincaid grade levels equate to the American school grades. So:

American Grade	British school Year	Approximate age	Approximate Qualifications level.
Kindergarten	1	5/6	
1	2	6/7	
2	3	7/8	
3	4	8/9	
4	5	9/10	
5	6	10/11	
6	7	11/12	
7	8	12/13	
8	9	13/14	
9	10	14/15	Non Qualified school leaver/ GNVQ Foundation/ NVQ1
10	11	15/16	GCSE – Level 2
11	12	16/17	AS level
12	13	17/18	A2 level – Level 3

Beyond these grades the readability level would be considered highly technical and graded at undergraduate, graduate and higher degree levels.

If you find your scores are very high, too high for the learners' reading levels, then try to simplify and shorten sentences and reduce the number of multi-syllabic words.

One example of the many texts that may need to be rewritten for learners with a literacy level less than Level 2 is the instructions that are provided by Microsoft Help, precisely the sorts of tools learners might be directed towards to solve their ICT difficulties. Take, for example, the instructions on using the spell checker. This text is very dense and full of technical and multi-syllabic words:

Ways to check spelling and grammar

Microsoft Word provides several ways to check spelling and grammar:

Automatically correct spelling and grammar To fix spelling and grammatical errors without having to confirm each correction, use the AutoCorrect feature. For example, if you type definately and then type a space or other punctuation, AutoCorrect replaces it with 'definitely.' AutoCorrect can make corrections that are generated by the spelling checker's main dictionary, and by a list of built-in AutoCorrect entries. You can easily add your own AutoCorrect entries or remove unwanted ones.

Automatically check spelling and grammar as you type To check for spelling and grammatical errors 'behind the scenes,' use automatic spelling and grammar checking. As you type, the spelling and grammar checkers check the text, and then mark possible errors with wavy underlines. To correct an error, display a shortcut menu and select the correction you want. If you find the wavy underlines distracting, you can temporarily hide the underlines until you're ready to make corrections.

Check spelling and grammar all at once You can check for spelling and grammatical errors, and then confirm each correction. This method is useful if you want to postpone proofing a document until after you finish editing it.

Check the spelling and grammar of text in another language To check text in another language, you need to install the spelling and grammar tools for that language, and make sure the language is enabled for editing. Thereafter, Word automatically detects the language in your documents, and uses the correct spelling and grammar tools.

Photo: Sue Parkins, NIACE

A readability check on this text shows that it comes up as Flesch–Kincaid Grade level 12. The reader would be expected to be able to read or be educated to A-level or Level 3 standard.

Chunking text

Large amounts of dense text and long, complicated lists of instructions may challenge deaf learners, particularly those who have experienced delayed language acquisition.

Teachers simplifying the text, or breaking it down into smaller manageable 'chunks' of information, can overcome some of these challenges. The use of clearer fonts and appropriate illustrations, including pictures or video clips, can improve readability. Putting text into text boxes and using colour or highlighters to denote different aspects of learning may also help.

Font

Font types and font sizes can make a huge impact on the readability of text. Fonts that use serifs, the curly ends of letters on letters such as h and m, tend to be less easy to read, especially for people experiencing reading difficulties and those with specific learning difficulties such as dyslexia. Some readers prefer Ariel or Comic Sans as opposed to Times New Roman, not only because they are serif-free ('sans serif') but because all their letters resemble the familiar handwritten forms – compare 'g' and 'a' in the examples below

Comic Sans: g a

Times New Roman: g a

Photo: Sue Parkins, NIACE

Upper or lower case letters

The constant use of uppercase letters (capitals) also reduces readability. All capital letters appear in a uniform height, and letters such as p, q, and g lose their distinctive shape. This means that words also lose their shape and become less recognisable.

The shapes of individual words are more easily recognised

THE SHAPES OF INDIVIDUAL WORDS ARE MORE DIFFICULT TO RECOGNISE

Using digital images

Digital images are essential elements of resources to support deaf learners. Visual reference materials can be:

> stored on a PC or CD

> printed and kept in a reference file or laminated and used as a class resource

> inserted into handouts

> inserted into presentations

> used in a range of software

> placed into online learning materials – see Hot Potatoes, page 51.

Case study: Digital prospectus

Bolton LEA has recorded samples of classes and images of learners participating in learning on to a DVD-based prospectus of learning opportunities. These images can be set up to play in public areas such as libraries and health centres. Similarly, teaching sessions can be recorded on to a DVD, which can be useful for learners who require time to review each session's activities in their own time.

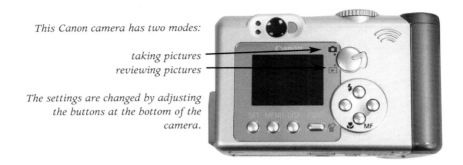

This Canon camera has two modes:

taking pictures
reviewing pictures

The settings are changed by adjusting the buttons at the bottom of the camera.

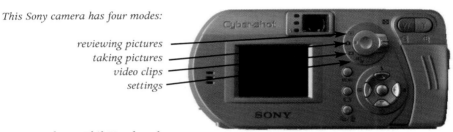

This Sony camera has four modes:

reviewing pictures
taking pictures
video clips
settings

Photo: Phil Hardcastle

Digital still cameras

These provide quick and easy access to relevant images for customised hard copy and computer based resources. They offer support for language development, understanding of concepts and processes, and revision. There are also no copyright issues. If you intend to photograph learners, make sure that you have their permission.

> For more on digital cameras see the NIACE e-guideline *Digital cameras in teaching and learning*, by Phil Hardcastle (2005).

Photo Story 3 for Windows

Photo stories are excellent teaching tools and also provide ways for deaf learners to work with a primarily visual medium. Photo Story 3 for Windows is an easy to use piece of free software from Microsoft. It can turn a series of photographs into a useful teaching resource or act as a creative tool for learners. The photographs can appear animated as the automatic or selected pan and zoom options create a video feel. There are different transitions and options to add text and, for some learners, recorded voice and music.

The tutor can take photographs of such activities as a cookery demonstration and add key words and phrases. A learner can keep a photographic record of a process they have worked through, some artwork for example, and then run the images together to demonstrate their progress. A really lively way to celebrate achievement.

For more on PhotoStory, including some examples of good practice, see: **www.microsoft.com/windowsxp/using/digitalphotography/ photostory/default.mspx**

PowerPoint storyboards

Inserting images into PowerPoint slides is useful for a range of educational purposes including the support of language and cognitive development, sequencing skills, practical skills, following processes etc. Images can be combined with text, AutoShapes such as lines, arrows, flowcharts, speech and thought bubbles. They can be printed and presented as individual pages or presented as books. They can have spaces for writing and laminated for learners who need an easy-clean facility to enable them to re-try.

On-screen use means that pictures, objects and text that make up a slide can be animated in various ways: they can be brought onto the screen on a mouse click or on automatic timer. Animations give the option of discussing an image before text, AutoShape or another image is brought on screen, giving valuable time to assimilate information, discuss or predict. This can be especially useful to deaf learners who may require a controlled introduction of elements of learning.

For more on PowerPoint: **http://office.microsoft.com/en-us/ workessentials/CH102026781033.aspx**

PowerPoint also offers the facility to create a live text box within a presentation. This means that teacher or learner can add typed text whilst the information is displayed on screen.

Big Book Maker

This software supports the production of downloadable e-books that include text, images and sound. It was originally designed to support young children but it has been used to create e-books for adult learners and there is tremendous potential for use with deaf learners. It is free of charge if used for educational purposes. Books can be tailor made for on-screen learning that allows the learner to select from a contents page and leaf through pages on a mouse click. It can provide very supportive and accessible reference materials for independent learning

For further information visit **www.aclearn.net**

Clicker 5

Clicker 5 uses a split screen with a word processor at the top and grid at the bottom. The grids are prepared by teachers to provide letters, words, phrases or pictures to support learners whilst they are working. There is a good picture library to which you can add your own images.

The grids can offer significant support to deaf learners who lack sophisticated reading and writing skills or who may need help with subject-specific vocabulary.

There is an excellent speech engine that enables text to be spoken, and it doesn't sound like a computer!

www.cricksoft.com/uk/products/clicker/guide.htm

Digital video

A video clip can explain a process and offer signed support/explanation or perhaps a signed keywords dictionary. BSL clips can be inserted into PowerPoint and combined with text. Video also gives BSL users a way of communicating that can then be translated into English.

Specialised video cameras will produce high-quality results but we can still create useful resources without them: still cameras often have the facility to take short video clips, and webcams offer a cheap and satisfactory alternative to more expensive dedicated video cameras.

Case Study: Capturing signed words with a still camera with video facility

A teacher wanted a quick solution to vocabulary issues facing a deaf learner. She arranged for a Communication Support Worker to meet her and took video clips of signed words.

The room was well lit with natural light coming from a large window. The CSW stood against a plain, light background and wore dark clothing. The camera was set up on a tripod and framed the upper half of the body to capture the signing completely.

The teacher did not want to edit clips, so they formulated and rehearsed a start and finish protocol. Each sign was videoed as follows: the CSW stood with arms at his side whilst the teacher counted down '5, 4, 3, 2, 1'; at '1' the camera was started and the CSW made the sign; when the sign was completed, he put his arms by his side and the camera was stopped.

Each sign in turn was recorded in this way and the clips could then be used as they were.

Windows Movie Maker is video editing software that comes with Windows XP and offers a basic, but useful, means of editing film clips or creating a movie. Likewise, iMovie is useful video editing software created by Apple Computers for the Macintosh.

www.microsoft.com/windowsxp/using/moviemaker/default.mspx

www.apple.com/support/imovie/

There may be better software that came with a video camera, or your organisation may have purchased specialist software. But even if all you have is a webcam or still camera that takes video clips, material can be edited or used as filmed.

Webcams

A webcam can display something that is happening in real time in a classroom or anywhere around the world. There are live streaming webcams set up in public places and museums that can support elements of learning.

A few examples of webcams:

- Natural History Museum:
http://www.nhm.ac.uk/kids-only/naturecams/
- Inverary Maritime Experience
http://www.inveraray.tv/
- Panama Canal
http://www.pancanal.com/eng/photo/camera-java.html
- Antarctica
http://www.aad.gov.au/asset/webcams/mawson/default.asp

Case Study: Using a webcam for live video streaming

A teacher wanted to demonstrate how to do an embroidery stitch. She was aware that the experience could be enhanced for her deaf learner, a BSL user. A webcam was trained on her hands whilst she accomplished the stitch and it was relayed in real time to the screen. As the teacher worked she talked and the Communication Support Worker stood by the screen and signed what the teacher was saying. This meant that the deaf learner was able to see the working and explanation side by side. This would have been very difficult if she was required to focus closely on the teacher's work.

The teacher also recorded clips so that she could replay them as needed.

Some webcams have software that will produce time-lapse sequences and animations. These add to the learning experience for any deaf learners whose dominant sense is sight, whose preferred learning style is visual and who is used to reading visual information.

Video conferencing

There are various ways of delivering video conferencing, from the simple and cheap webcam sitting on top of your computer to very expensive and sophisticated equipment.

There is a wide range of possibilities for combining messaging systems with digital images. Adding a webcam into a messaging system, such as MSN or Skype, can enhance the communication, particularly for deaf people. Sign language users can sign to each other and an interpreter can interpret for speakers and sign language users.

More on Skype:
www.skype.com/intl/en-gb/download/features/videocalling/

The better the conferencing equipment and connection, the better the experience can be. Video conferencing is an ideal medium for BSL users and can bring together individuals or disparate groups for a social chat or a shared learning experience. This can particularly support learners in areas where there are few or no other deaf learners and who may feel socially isolated.

Video conferencing enables teachers to link with establishments such as art galleries and museums, to participate in remote visits and facilitate distance learning.

Case Study: Improving conference accessibility

To facilitate the participation of deaf learners and tutors, a camera was focused on a signer at a formal presentation in a large hall with a substantial audience. A screen next to the speaker displayed the signed interpretation, enabling deaf members of the audience to see both speaker and interpreter whilst having the freedom to sit where they chose.

Digital microscopes

These also vary in price. The most basic are webcams attached to a simple microscope or magnifying lens. Whatever the level of complexity of the set-up, resulting images can be displayed effectively on a screen or whiteboard as an aid to visual learning. The learner is freed from having to switch attention from viewing through a microscope to accessing whatever the teacher is saying. The process of relating the image to the explanation is easier and quicker.
www.microscopy-uk.org.uk/full_menu.html

Scanning images and objects

Scanners offer a quick and cheap means of getting images into an electronic form to insert into on screen and printed resources. Remember that you will need to observe copyright issues if you are capturing images from other sources. Your scanner may be able to differentiate between text and images, allowing you to save images for editing and insert text into a word processing package so that you can make changes.

It is also possible to scan objects. For example, an art teacher talking about texture may scan objects or fabrics to demonstrate this. When scanning objects take care to protect the scanner bed.

Finding images on the web

Search engines such as Google and Yahoo Search will support the search of images only. Type your subject into the box and click on the **Images** tab above, then search. You will also find a number of animated gif files on the Web which will show moving images. Particularly useful are those that show how things work, for example the heart or an erupting volcano. Ensure you observe copyright laws.

> For more on the WorldWide Web for adult learners, see the NIACE e-guideline *Online resources in the classroom*, by Alan Clarke and Claudia Hesse (2005).

Linking to websites

It is not always necessary to save images or insert them into resources, you can prepare links to websites to use during a session – providing you have a reliable connection. By using a hyperlink you can display a web address, an image or an object that, when clicked, on will open up a specified site.

Case study: Using Web images to explain volcanoes

A tutor had traditionally used print materials to explain what caused volcanic eruptions but found that this was not inclusive practice for his deaf learners. They needed to see the pictures and lip read at the same time and this was not possible if they were looking at an image in a book.

He researched supportive images on the Web because he felt that a few images could help explain more quickly than a lot of words that may need careful repetition. He found useful photographs and animations which he either inserted into a presentation or created links to pages on specific sites and introduced them to satellite views of volcanoes via Google Earth (don't zoom in too close if you want to get the best view!).

He sat with his laptop, facing the learners, and so was able to show the image behind him on a screen and enable learners to look at the image and his face. He could see when they were watching him and could easily gain their attention when required.

He directed learners to a site of links to webcams at volcanoes around the world: **http://www.volcanolive.com/volcanocams.html**

Flash

Software that enables teachers to create their own animations tailored to support deaf learners in specific curriculum areas. Training in its use is essential.

Buying images

Images are available to purchase on CD or downloaded from the Internet.

Change Picture Bank, for example, is a collection of drawn simple pictures designed to support text for adults with learning difficulties. Their simplicity makes them relatively easy to understand. Illustrations in the Change Picture Bank have been categorised under various headings such as work, emotions, people, objects and ICT. These symbols are available as a software package from: **www.changepeople.co.uk**

It is important to use illustrations that illuminate the text. Amusing or entertaining illustrations that do not work as visual cues could be distracting or even confusing for learners trying to extract meaning from them.

Symbols

Symbol systems have been developed to support literacy. For example Widget software's 'Writing with Symbols' software system automatically places symbols above each word, so that either those reading or writing have a better meaning of individual words. The system is sophisticated enough to allow the user to differentiate between words that look the same, such as saw or spell, or sound the same, such as hare and hair.

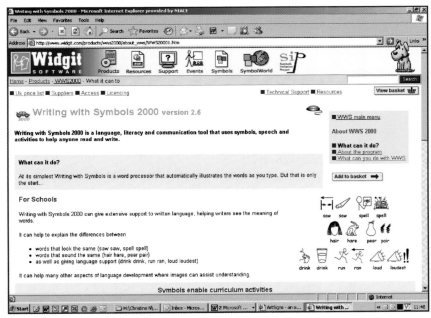

See www.widgit.com/products/wws2000/index.htm

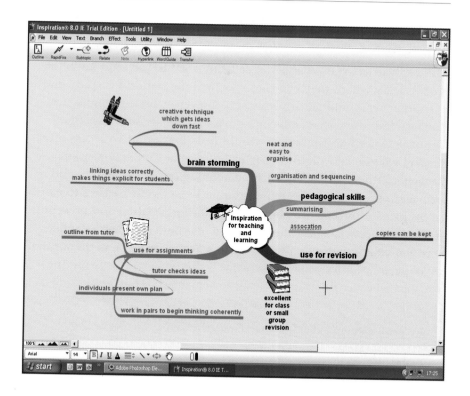

Mind mapping/concept mapping

Visual learners, including many deaf learners, benefit from a graphic organisation of thoughts that supports the management and organisation of information. Mind mapping is basically a stream of consciousness approach to note taking and planning, using colour and graphics to show relationships. The maps can grow and learners can add different paths and subpaths at any point. It is a highly visual way to record information and concepts, and by giving a shape to a topic, causes the topic to become more memorable. Specialist software is not necessary as mind maps can be drawn by hand, but technology helps with presentation, revision and storage for recall at a later date. Interactive whiteboards (IWB) provide an excellent set up for creating mind maps, as can using IWB software with the appropriate tablet to facilitate handwriting away from the screen. There are specialist software packages available:
Inspiration **www.inspiration.com/productinfo/index.cfm**
or FreeMind
http://freemind.sourceforge.net/wiki/index.php/Main_Page

49

Using the Internet

All deaf learners should experience using the Internet and learn the processes by which they can find specific information for study and to support work and leisure activities. However, literacy issues may make surfing the web a challenging exercise for those whose first language is not English or who would need extra time to access often densely written and high-level-readability text. Tutors who want learners to find specific information should consider structure and support options. It may be more productive to guide learners to more accessible sites or take the most significant information and present it in a less complex and text heavy way. This could be made available after the session or as an alternative to a Web search, or in the form of a Webquest . Tutors need to ask what is the purpose of surfing the Net, and whether it is the best way to achieve that purpose.

For more on the WorldWide Web for adult learners, see the NIACE *e-guideline Online resources in the classroom*, by Alan Clarke and Claudia Hesse (2005).

Creating interactive materials

Interactive whiteboard software

Interactive Whiteboards come with dedicated software that is specifically designed for interactivity. Visual and kinaesthetic learners gain from being able to manipulate what is on the board. Practitioners should investigate which software is in use within their organisation and how it can be accessed to create resources to support deaf learners. Check that the latest version is installed, as software is likely to have been improved and may offer access to more images than an older version. You may also have access to curriculum-specific animated files that help explain something specific, such as measuring angles or how to measure voltage using a voltmeter.
There are scores of such animations for SMART products listed here:
http://education.smarttech.com/ste/en-US/Ed+Resource/Software+Resources/Notebook+collections/

'Hot Potatoes'

Hot Potatoes is a software application for creating web-based quizzes and other activities. It enables practitioners to prepare gap-fill (cloze) exercises;

> questions with multiple choice answers;
> short answer activities;
> matching and ordering exercises;
> crosswords.

Communication issues make it essential to check whether a deaf learner has been able to access teaching; Hot Potatoes enables the production of quick tests that focus on elements of learning, testing understanding and tracking learners' progress. This makes it easier to identify learners who may be missing, or have misunderstood, significant information, and encourages tutors to change their teaching to meet the needs of deaf learners.

Hot Potatoes software is not freeware, but it is free of charge for people working for publicly funded non-profit-making educational institutions who make their pages available on the web. Other users need to purchase a licence.

Hot Potatoes: **http://hotpot.uvic.ca/**

Case study – Quick tests

A tutor of floristry techniques devised quick tests using Hot Potatoes and Form Fields in Word. These are particularly useful to assess what the deaf learners have understood, avoiding communication issues that may be stressful. They are completed at the individual learner's pace and the tutor is able to provide the relevant feedback and support.

She is hoping to develop a bank of resources that she can call up with other learners.

Electronic voting systems

Usefully employed to track individual learning, a voting system is a set of remote voting pads that used to respond to questions set by the teacher. Questions can include supportive images for deaf learners The learner may be provided with immediate feedback on their individual handset and/or by results displayed on screen. Questions and answer options are generally brief and clearly presented, there is an element of fun and, most importantly, the deaf learner is not required to write or speak and the nature of their response can remain anonymous, with only the tutor being able to identify weaknesses in learning.

Photo: Nick Hayes

'ClozePro' by Crick Software

This software is specifically designed to create a range of cloze activities. The format is clear and user-friendly, providing grids from which users select individual words or phrases to fill the spaces. There is a bank of good, clear images to offer visual clues, to which you can add your own images, and software speech is available for those who have sufficient residual hearing and want to both hear and see the words.

ClozePro also has the facility to track a learner's progress to see what prompts he or she used before selecting a final answer, and a range of accessibility options.
ClozePro: http://www.cricksoft.com/uk/

The Microsoft Office Suite

PowerPoint, Word and Excel can all be used to create simple interactive exercises. To be effective they need to be well designed and provide good feedback to add value to the learning process. These activities can also be made available online via learning platforms to provide reinforcing exercises outside the class teaching time.

Supporting the deaf writer

There will be some deaf learners who will benefit from software that supports the writing process. Word-processing packages have tools to check spelling and grammar, but these will not be very helpful if the learner has experienced delayed language acquisition and is still developing literacy skills. Scaffolding tools, word banks, predictive word-processing software, editing and re-drafting facilities can offer good support and take some of the strain out of writing.

Writing frames provide learners with a structure in which to record their thoughts. These can be created using word processing packages. The Forms toolbar in Microsoft Word is a useful way of creating frames. Providing a structure can free the learner to concentrate on content. Graphics can be added to offer visual cues.

Penfriend XP

'Penfriend' can be used to support deaf learners who find spelling a challenge. It predicts the words a learner may want to use as the letters are typed and will build up a memory of a user's most frequently used words to make prediction faster. Teachers can add curriculum-specific word banks.

Penfriend XP: **www.penfriend.ltd.uk/products/pfxp.shtml**

WordBar

This Crick software enables teachers to prepare grids of words that sit at the bottom of the computer screen. Each grid may contain the relevant vocabulary for a particular aspect of learning and a learner can toggle between grids and insert a word into their text simply by clicking on it.

This facility may help those who have difficulty remembering how to spell a word. They may remember initial letters or recognise the pattern of a word; the on-screen resource cuts down the stress of a writing activity.

Deaf learners with sufficient residual hearing could also benefit from the high-quality speech software that enables them to hear the words before they select them.

WordBar: **http://www.cricksoft.com/uk/products/wordbar/**

We should also encourage learners to be creative in their response and provide them with the skills and facilities to use images and visual cues in their own work.

Learning platforms

A learning platform is a web-based facility that provides opportunities for teachers and learners to access materials around their curriculum area of interest. They often provide online discussion forums and chat facilities that can be used to reinforce learning outside the classroom. One type of learning platform is

'Moodle'. (http://moodle.org). Teachers load learning materials on to the site; other teachers or learners with an interest in the same topic can access them. It can be really helpful to both the teacher and learner to see how other teachers present content

Teachers and learners can now share and develop better resources through the use of learning platforms. Managers and practitioners need to develop a culture of sharing that enables those whose collective aim is to educate and enrich the lives of all adults to contribute to providing quality resources that can be adapted and modified. This would be an invaluable resource for minority groups such as deaf learners.

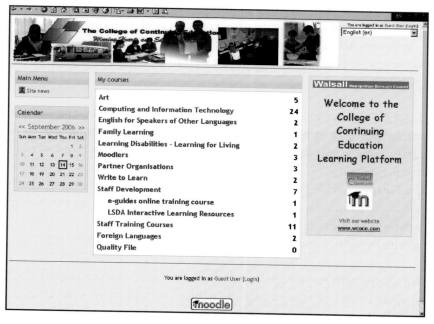

If appropriate, it is possible to create areas specifically for deaf learners that may address both curriculum and social needs,

References and further reading

Action on Deafness (2005) *BSL Tutor support pack*, Leicester.

Anderberg, P. and Jonsson, B. (2005) 'Being there' in *Disability & society*, Vol 20, No 7, December 2005, 719–734.

Clarke, A. and Hesse, C. (2005) *Online Resources for the Classroom*, Leicester, NIACE.

Department for Education and Skills (2006) ESOL *Access for All: Guidance on making the Adult ESOL curriculum accessible*. Part 1', London, DfES.

Hardcastle, P (2005) *Digital cameras in teaching and learning*, Leicester, NIACE.

Photo: Sue Parkins, NIACE

Glossary

e -learning 'learning supported or enhanced through the application of Information and Communications Technology (ICT).' (e-learning Standards Lifelong Learning UK/FENTO, LSDA, 2005)

E-guide An E-Guide is someone who has completed the E-Guides staff development programme. The E-Guides programme is designed for staff who deliver adult learning to develop their use of e-learning across the curriculum. The programme aims to increase the use of e-learning in ACL through developing the skills and knowledge of E-Guides so that they are able to support colleagues from all subjects in their use of technology in teaching and learning. Each E-Guide is encouraged to develop an action plan for cascading their skills and knowledge for their local situation. E-Guides contribute to raising the quality of teaching and learning throughout their organisation.

e-guideline The NIACE e-guidelines series provides guidance and support, accessible advice and useful examples of good practice for adult learning practitioners wishing to use digital technology in all its forms to attract and support adult learners.

Medical model of disability The medical model sees that the 'problems' of disability as being located in the individual. It is the individual who has to adapt, or adjust to be included in society. See 'Social Model of Disability'.

MSN Messenger Is an instant messaging service and part of the Microsoft Network collection of services

Skype is a peer-to-peer internet telephone network. The system includes free voice and video conferencing,

Social model of disability By contrast with the medical model, the social model shifts the focus from the individual to society. Identifying how attitudes, systems, the built environment and policies create barriers to inclusion and participation.

SMOG (Simplified Measure Of Gobbledygook) A score/measure of readability based upon assessing indicators of complexity, e.g. sentence length and numbers of multi-syllable words.